Small Crimes

ANHINGA PRESS

SMALL CRIMES

POEMS

ANDREA JURJEVIĆ

2015 PHILIP LEVINE PRIZE FOR POETRY
Selected by C. G. Hanzlicek

ANHINGA PRESS
TALLAHASSEE, FLORIDA 2017

Cover Image: *Woman with Homunculus* by Egon Schiele
Private Collection, Courtesy Richard Nagy Ltd., London.
Author photograph: Forest McMullin
Design, production: Jay Snodgrass
Type Styles: Adobe Caslon Pro and Mrs Eaves OT

Library of Congress Cataloging-in-Publication Data
Small Crimes by Andrea Jurjević — First Edition
ISBN — 978-1-934695-50-0
Library of Congress Cataloging Card Number — 2016952107

Anhinga Press Inc. is a nonprofit corporation dedicated wholly to the publication and appreciation of fine poetry and other literary genres.

For personal orders, catalogs, and information, write to:

ANHINGA PRESS
P.O. Box 3665 • Tallahassee, Florida 32315
Website: www.anhingapress.org • Email: info@anhingapress.org

Published in the United States by Anhinga Press
Tallahassee, Florida • First Edition, 2017

for my parents

THE PHILIP LEVINE PRIZE FOR POETRY

The annual competition for the Philip Levine Prize for Poetry is sponsored and administered by the M.F.A. Program in Creative Writing at California State University, Fresno.

2015
Andrea Jurjević
Small Crimes
Selected by C. G. Hanzlicek

2014
Christine Poreba
Rough Knowledge
Selected by Peter Everwine

2013
Chelsea Wagenaar
Mercy Spurs the Bone
Selected by Philip Levine

2012
Barbara Brinson Curiel
Mexican Jenny and Other Poems
Selected by Cornelius Eady

2011
Ariana Nadia Nash
Instructions for Preparing Your Skin
Selected by Denise Duhamel

2010
Lory Bedikian
The Book of Lamenting
Selected by Brian Turner

2009
Sarah Wetzel
Bathsheba Transatlantic
Selected by Garrett Hongo

2008
Shane Seely
The Snowbound House
Selected by Dorianne Laux

2007
Neil Aitken
The Lost Country of Sight
Selected by C.G. Hanzlicek

2006
Lynn Aarti Chandhok
The View from Zero Bridge
Selected by Corrinne Clegg Hales

2005
Roxane Beth Johnson
Jubilee
Selected by Philip Levine

2002
Steven Gehrke
The Pyramids of Malpighi
Selected by Philip Levine

2001
Fleda Brown
Breathing In, Breathing Out
Selected by Philip Levine

CONTENTS

ACKNOWLEDGEMENTS

This book exists because of a series of gifts.

Heartfelt thanks to the editors of the following magazines where these poems first appeared, sometimes in earlier versions:

Anderbo: "Back When"

Barrelhouse: "While the Backwoods Burned"

Berkeley Poetry Review: "You Came Here Through Istanbul" and "Storm" (now "Crows' Voices")

Best New Poets and Verse Wisconsin: "For Yugoslavia's More Fortunate `Ones"

Chattahoochee Review: "When at Moonlight You Knock on My Door"

EPOCH: "Bluesman Wept and Midnight Couldn't Hide It"

Falling Star Magazine: "Lament With Milkweed"

Flycatcher: "Nocturne in Black, and Lacy-Red Arils of Nutmeg"

Harpur Palate: "Limp Saints" (now "Early War Years")

I-70 Review: "Memphis Aubade" and "Sparring With Unanswered Phone Calls"

Midwest Quarterly: "Dissolution" and "Maria"

Missouri Review: "Cinema Verite: A Love Story," "In the Absence of Grass," "Sarajevo Cycle: 1992-1996," "The First Time," "Wafer-Like and White" and "Would It Surprise You I Don't Like Mornings"

Poet Lore: "An Old Photo of You Taken in a Gin Mill Outside Zagreb" (now "An Old Photo of You Taken in a Gin Mill Outside Our Peninsula")

Radar Poetry: "Hotel Scandinavia"

Sequestrum: "Hands"

Southern Humanities Review: "Threshold"

Poydras Review: "Thievery"

Prime Number Magazine: "Gifts for the Past" and "I Close My Hand, Stars Fall Through My Fingers"

Raleigh Review: "Aubade"

Rag Literary Journal: "Elevation"

Rappahannock Review: "Small Crimes" and "Divorce" (now "Pomegranate")

Slipstream: "Peeling an Orange"

Sixfold: "It was a Large Wardrobe, From My 4-Foot Perspective" and "Love Boat"

Spoon River Poetry Review: "Too Educated"

The Journal: "Aubade With the Marking Scent of Tobacco, Sweat, Sores"

The Sow's Ear Poetry Review: "English Lesson"

Town Creek Poetry: "While Painting a Fall Landscape, I Imagine"

Tor House Newsletter: "Men From Camps"

TriQuarterly: "Skirt Dripping Sea"

Thank you to Kim Addonizio and Robinson Jeffers Tor House Foundation for awarding the poem "Men From Camps" with the 2013 Robinson Jeffers Prize, and to Elliot Ruchowitz-Roberts for his hospitality and friendship.

I would like to thank my teachers and mentors at Georgia State University's MFA program, especially David Bottoms, Beth Gylys, Leon Stokesbury, Matthew Roudane, and Pearl McHaney. I would also like to thank my friends for their inspirational push, enthusiasm, and honest feedback, particularly to Rupert Fike, Diya Chaudhuri, Jenny Brown, Hank Backer, Christine Swint, Kristin Robertson,

Brian Heston, Karen Holmes and the Side Door Poets. Thank you to James Thomas Miller for flaming the initial word-fire. Thank you to those who shared their love — you know who you are, the very beat of these poems.

I am also grateful to the Sewanee Writers' Conference for the Tennessee Williams scholarship, the guidance of Sidney Wade and B. H. Fairchild, and to my Sewanee friends for their sharp wit and their terrific spunk. Sincere gratitude also goes to the Hambidge Center, and the Fulton County for the Arts and Culture Fellowship, and their gift of time and solitude.

Finally, my deep gratitude goes to C. G. Hanzlicek, and everyone at Fresno State University, for awarding *Small Crimes* the Philip Levine prize. Massive thank you to Anhinga Press, and especially to wonderful Jay Snodgrass, for the making of this book.

Most of all, I thank my sons for the joy, and my parents for the seeker's spirit.

Small Crimes

It snakes behind me, this invisible chain gang —
the aliases, your many faces peopling

that vast hotel, the past. What did we learn?

— Lynda Hull

FOR YUGOSLAVIA'S MORE FORTUNATE ONES

You killed time, and your livers, under viaducts,
vigilantes of underpasses in thick vinegar haze,

puking by the roadside over tin foil, empty bottles,
toilet paper tubes, buttercups, morning glories.

Days welded. Onions sweated in wood crates
at the market. Fish gutted, their scales

thrown back to the sea — that lax bluish rag
between the port and smokestacks. The burn off.

You watched busses start routes at 5 a.m.,
considered yourselves above the proletariat

that waited somber under fiberglass stops
for the busses' concertina doors to take them,

then watched those soot-crusted vehicles
bend through intestinal streets — past posters

of Yugoslav bands, their multiethnic disco quaver,
past the greenery of dumpsters. You, vigilante

drifters at school parks under the carob trees,
habitually fucking on beds of sun-scorched papers.

And you, stooped by the betting shop — on its walls
the fixed smile of Lady D, yellowed centerfolds,

Sabrina splashing about in her white bandeau bikini.
Remember that Roma boy who, for years, offered

Dobra pička[1] to passersby, his sister — a reasonably priced
premenstrual pussy — the two of them, arms linked,

beautiful together, like two black orchids.

1 See Glossary for Foreign Terms

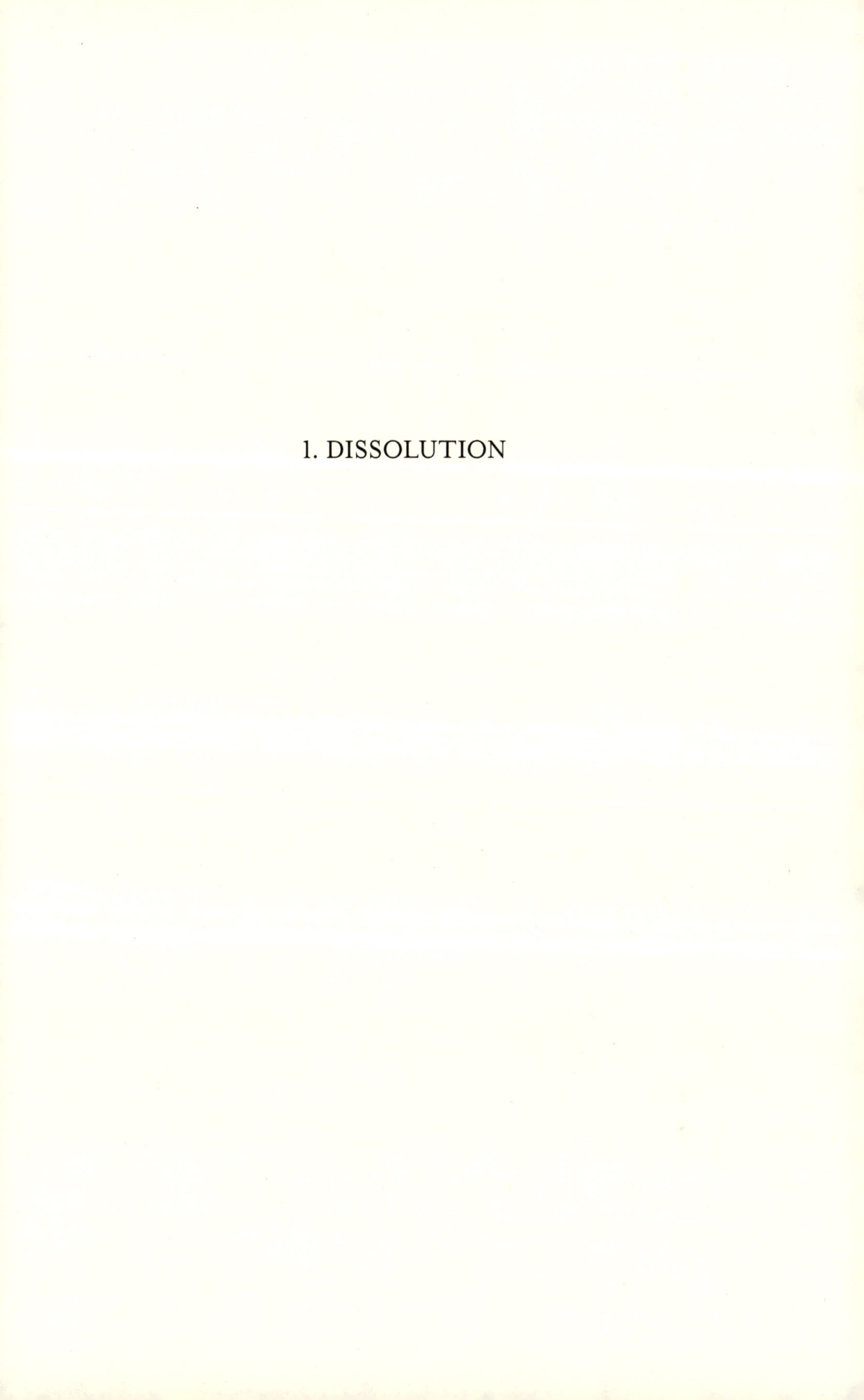

1. DISSOLUTION

WOULD IT SURPRISE YOU I DON'T LIKE MORNINGS

How bright the bombs must have looked
as the dawn stretched thin across the hills,
shrapnel sleeting on the terracotta roofs.
For another sixty years, every time she'd step out
of her bungalow, she'd face the monument —
ten yards ahead, the shell of her old house now storage:
trunks of fabrics, potatoes sprouting in mesh bags,
the stink of drying prosciutto, pigs' feet. I like to think
she'd always turn left to the solid stone well,
1902 chiseled on its base, planters rusting
(*pomodori pelati* cans), the screen of blue grape vines
taut like boat ropes overgrown with moss. I remember
my aunts grumbling under that shade and to the right,
in bell-bottoms, my uncle slouching in a plastic chair —
long sideburns, the sheen of scissors in Mom's hands
and the graying tufts falling on grass like ashes. I remember
Mom's cheeks being higher than the hills, Nona's breasts
pulled and vein-ridden like grapeskin, and Nono
singing and twirling with Linda, his dog.
No one spoke about the ruin, no one mentioned her two boys
found in the woods, slaughtered with partisans,
their oldest brother sniped while passing a window
in his room at the general hospital. No one remembered
her first husband's name, or the name of the neighbor
who called him out at 5 a.m., then returned two hours later
for coffee and grappa she had to offer, her Italian husband
prostrate in a grove, executed with other suspected
Fascists. No one talked about how that was the house
Germans bombed and how that morning the shadows
must have been audible moments before the planes —
Jesus clamoring on the cross above the front door,
the tremor like no other, the dust. Perhaps a cry.

Nona thrown under her Singer sewing machine,
its treadle in perpetual up-down, the fabric slipping
and the baby, another boy, crushed by the roof beams.
Then the silence. Like our secrecy. They say joy is a choice
but no one mentions victims. So, hushed it stays. Back home
you spread, almost asleep. I make here there, glide over
your forbidden back and lip the scar under your ear. We do this
each night, never let the daylight see it. Victims ruin it.

MARIA

— Post World War II, Croatia

No toys. Only birds and goats. And no nice stories.
Mama in black, always down. She was a good woman,
though, and Tata in high spirits, usually lit on *loza.*

For Christmas, we'd hang candy on the tree,
eat it straight away. Donation boxes sent from Torino
were our presents — raw coffee beans, socks, walnuts.

The corn-husk mattress, the bed in the kitchen
by the stove, ice like milk skin on the window,
and the three of us, sisters, curled like newborn cats.

There was no TV, no radio, but a gramophone
the Italian army had left behind. When adults got drunk,
they'd put some old record on, unhook the accordion,

belt out folk songs. I never cared for the Beatles.
No TV, no radio then — we lived in dark.
I was born in a *štala*, you know.

We'd walk for an hour to school — five kilometers.
By the time your shoes would dry and ice
would melt off your brows, you'd get arthritis.

Calligraphy: fine lines up, thick ones down.
Math was disgusting. My teacher's still alive. He's disgusting —
and his long, palm-cutting rod. Locked us up hungry

once after class, gave us extra work, went out for drinks.
My sister teased us from the window, *Trouble, trouble,*
what ya doin? Next year, he became the director of Goli Otok,

the political prison. But we felt free, ran around the village,
raced after the army trucks that would dust up the road,
tanks that patrolled every day, Yugoslav Army.

Mama had one cow that wasn't normal. Chased
everyone, tried to butt neighbors in their backs,
except for Mama. They'd walk together like best friends.

She was in our yard one day when this woman, Pepa,
passed by — the cow, all instant rage, charged after her,
up the lane, through cabbages and grapes.

Pepa was hysterical, ran and bolted herself into that *štala*
I was born in. Everyone watched. The cow was furious,
kept goring its crooked door. Mama had to shoot her.

TOO EDUCATED

After Momo Kapor

His older sister, bereft in black, puts the *džezva*
  on the stove. Her hand, the hand of a chaste girl,
brushes the wildflowers on the tablecloth. Yet in the life

of any older sister there is some long-gone man,
  or brother, whose photograph stretches horizontal
on the bottom of an empty praline box.

We sit around what remains: cracked linoleum tiles,
  chopped wood under the stove, a blinking 25 watt bulb
and a black & white TV. The metal clock ticks.

In hand-knit sweaters he fought for scholarships
  back when chicks used to peck black holes
under a walnut tree. The rolling Slavic tongue

and our manner of speaking left no trace in his prose,
  only disgust for rain, mud and summer dust — provinciality.
It's difficult to define this treachery,

and still, we drink sweet coffee and say,
  because of her, how beautiful the big world must be,
and all the nice, expected things about him.

IT WAS A LARGE WARDROBE, FROM MY 4-FOOT PERSPECTIVE

Deep enough to step into, touch lapels of his suits,
leather patch elbows of tweed jackets, ties lurking

through thin mod prints, hint of naphthalene and musk.
And Mom's feather-light blouses — slack polyester willows.

Rows of empty sleeves faced west, to the window
that framed the rugged Učka curving above the bay,

hazel-green as the eyes of a fox boa that Dad,
in one of his moments of bravado, had stolen

for Mom, and that she, of course, never wore. Once,
I saw those glassy eyes flash, as if at the dirt-brown stack

of scuffed briefcases at the bottom. Inside, Sister and I found,
stained, yet still glossy catalogs of '70s decadence —

page after frayed page of nudes running through poses.
Our lashes threshed at the sight of those glam-wantons —

and that dog. We'd seen sunbathers scattered across cliffs,
naked and lazy like fat beige gulls, and another time

we peeked through the keyhole at Grandpa bending
over a steaming bath, his body creased with sickness.

But that day we stared at something anarchic, circuslike —
big hollow O's of pink-frosted lips, eyes caked half-shut

with thick semen, and that puppy's innocent erection,
its mahogany fur as thick and brown as our pet setter's.

BACK WHEN I KNEW HOW TO SPEAK

After Olja Savičević Ivančević

Every time I'd utter a syllable,
    the rain wouldn't drum or rumble
against the asphalt of my street
    but double-spur my consonants.

Generally in a low, firm tone,
    and regardless of the weather,
the World Cup Finals,
    or barba Joško in the courtyard

ever-replacing rusted bolts
    on his skinny bicycle
while Mrs. Tomić would preen violets,
    petunias, smooth her varicose veins,

like a ten-ton truck
    storming through a tunnel,
I'd rise above giant TV antennas,
    white laundry clapping

like manic gloved hands,
    over chipped terracotta roofs,
above the Kvarner Bay
    and the Istrian peninsula.

I'd speak, in the same sentence,
    of fallen gods and funny bones,
about *Mamma Roma*,
    and *Les Quatre Cents Coups*.

And there, where the peninsula
            gives way to flatlands,
hillocks, sea-eaten caves,
            I once found a dump —

piles of unanswered and unsent notes —
stacked tall like stained toilet seats:
some playful couplets, horny invites,
a careful thank-you-but-no.

THE FIRST TIME

The smoke bathes my throat like a warm
frost-shadow. Borut, the red-faced Slovene,
grins hard, the capillaries of his wade-blue eyes
burst like bottle rockets, or like the peonies
around his homegrown pot. Local semirebels
surround him now, safety pins and crosses
dangle off their earlobes, the bucktoothed boy
lingers midsentence, someone laughs,
and I wonder if it's Borut's face or my age
that's amusing. I laugh because they seem happy,
huddled here under the lighthouse's blinking eye
as boats bob, slosh off the island. The tape player
spools out The Clash, The Dead Kennedys
until our voices double-back around the pier
and our talk loosens into silence: slow, clumsy
and plum with finale.
                                        Below, the village sleeps
like a giant gray baby, and the third-shift waiters
have cleared the patios. As I trod to my square
house — each footfall softer — *Jugo* drags
the Adriatic to the shore with no noise,
the salty foam pools around my ankles,
and my legs sink like two boat masts.

EARLY WAR YEARS

He undid her coat, talked, snaked about.
Rain dripped from the recessed doorway.

Vaffanculo, she swore, looking over her shoulder
at cork oaks weathered into still black worms.

He poured *mirto*, clean as baby breath,
into frosted glasses, talked, his words streaming

like schools of fish. She edged back —
No, cazzo, tu resti qui — and slammed the door.

His lip twitched, the glass spilled, his body stiff
like a Pompeian. That was an old movie on channel two.

Meanwhile, open windows let the clouds in —
muscular, fibrous — and the air reeked of ox dung.

An angel hung on a fishing line, limp
over the kitchen sill, above a soup bowl

filled with lake water and a floating lotus.
At the window, the pond-eyed gypsy

begged for coffee and sugar, her fingernails
clogged black with dried squid ink. She used to hum

Đelem đelem, and it seemed as if the melody
was the pulse of makeshift shanties —

scraps of ridged vinyl and burlap — her people
squatting around the ashes, horses roaming,

grubby children slingshotting tin cans distant as boats,
and a bull sauntering by, swinging his massive bullhood.

Later, in the city, after we mastered the curfews,
taping blankets to windows, the hysterical air raids,

we'd run out, strain our eyes guessing where the planes
were coming from. Men couldn't throw *boće* in the basement,

so they sat on beer crates, played *briškula* instead,
listened to the radio. Kids flocked to an old pinball machine,

learned how to flip-slam until their palms ached
and the worn metal ball was beat to a new shade of dull lead.

The soccer field gaped vacant and stubbly, the sea
tight-lipped. I'm not sure during which blackout

the old woman pulled the rosary out, but there it was,
on top of the folk music of patriotism, more drama.

IN THE ABSENCE OF GRASS

Cease-fire

Other than cypress columns, *macchia* and dried condoms
there isn't much interesting. Papier mâché cliffs

are flecked with gull scat, the sea tarp is still, and the sky
an apron sunk in dishwater. An odd tourist

sprawls on gravel like sourdough on a baker's slab,
flies court figs, the cracked-nipple fruit leaks,

and the fallen, tar-black flesh stinks of cheap wine.

I fiddle with a drop of sweat sliding down my belly —
it breaks like a man falling off a bridge.

Vukovar is a flabby flank cleaved by a switchblade;
Plitvice Lakes, a blooming minefield.

It's that muddy sweat that spreads like the popularity
of a new national hero. *Razbit ću ti pičku ustašku*!

he yells, then rapes any deserving cunt,
smirks through missing incisors, mindless,

he could be banging sacks of nails. He shoves meat
into a man's brindled beard — his grandson's liver —

later, strings their fingers on a necklace. A souvenir.

Meanwhile, the uncle I don't speak with passes time turning
lambs on a spit, and local hotels are infested with refugees.

In a couple of hours, I head to my summer job —
bar tending to dissipating locals and UN peacekeepers

who hold drinks better than peace. After rounds
of blindfolded pointing and gulping of hard liquor,

pug-snout bellowing YAAAHs!, they leave crumpled kunas
across warped tables. I put the cash aside for the owner,

and for a moment feel like a trained circus seal.

They like the Adriatic, they say, sun-rinsed girls, too,
but I suspect they like them anywhere they go.

Grandpa used to spend afternoons on his rattan chair
fixing nets. At dusk he'd unlash his white wooden boat

and row out the fairway to cast them. He repeated,
Red light at night, sailor's delight. Now dawns are scabbed —

each more vacant, hardened. Itchy and bothered,
like the itch of an amputee's foot. Afternoons, though,

still feel fine. We fool around by the shore,
roll pine needles in the absence of grass.

WAFER-LIKE AND WHITE

It's a self-defeating act, writing the 100-word bio,
but what about the footnotes? How my dad's bones

decay to chalk outside the curved palm of Kvarner Bay,
and how its forefinger still motions, lures back?

'92, the year before he died on the last day of summer,
how the war relieved the tired coastline of busloads

of Slovaks: no longer gawking around the Diocletian palace
in Split, no longer snapping their disposable Kodaks

at the salt-washed pillars of the arena in Pula, the ancient
game field getting its proper rest. As was the local

kiosk, with its metal lids pulled down, where as a kid,
on the first of each month, I used to stand on my toes,

clutch firmly to the sliding layers of newspapers
to buy cigarettes for Dad, and the new vacuum-packed

Erotika. How the markets yawned quietly, each shelf a showcase —
a handful of cookie boxes, a few plum preserves.

The radio station swaddled with sandbags. How later,
in a friend's house — perpetually under construction —

that ripe July Sunday morning spent inside warm brick walls,
a skinny boy also smoked Ronhills, and how cigarettes peeked

from the soft pack — wafer-like, white — on a single mattress
streaked with wine, a wrap-around skirt some uncle

brought from a trip to Nepal. How as two sixteen-year-olds
we held the room then, tight-lipped and cross-legged at first.

You smell like Indian apricots and introspection, he muttered.
I said nothing, his mouth later circling between the folds

of fabric, miming the sun pattern of the skirt print
in a breezy, wettish manner, like poisonous rain, and that hand,

the hand I thought I knew, the old hand I thought strong,
stopped his head, placed a punctuation before the end.

ELEVATION

The pines above the terraced churchyard
drip resin over stone roses and faceless cherubs
cresting the flat-tiered slabs

that glow as if in the presence of God.
Nearby, thriving in cornflower and ironweed,
a boat junkyard, more pines, their sticky breath

of decay, the crickets' toothed pitch.
Here a local sot pees into the *U* in Una
painted on the side of a white skiff

and gazes down at sunbathers —
the goat path dipping into the flat sea,
the penciled brows of gulls hovering in the sky.

He thinks of distant places he'll never see,
those smooth, glass-encased buildings,
the fox-gray scrawls of highways

that wind unlike his shore, jagged and broken
like chalk, and how there, he heard, the city lights
alone are worth menial labor, leaving

for good. He feels a tug in his neck, yearns
for a handful of cash, a sweet tourist ass.
He's watched them all his life,

carried their luggage sealed
with that good life, rented them umbrellas,
sold doughnuts with plum marmalade.

They come in couples. Sometimes with a child.
        She's German. Or Czech. Her name is Ingrid. Or Eva.
    Her thighs get dimpled from lying on the gravel.

She's shaved and you can almost see
        her clit, rosy and damp like the inside of a fig.
    Her voice isn't. She hates plums.

He lights a cigarette, palms his chin, swears,
        Gonna make this shit happen, and the smoke
swags down like falling hosiery,

clears in the warble of motorboats,
        in oars' muffled splashes, in the blue-braids
    and the nickel swirls of herring

where he'll wash the paint shavings
        out of his hands, the ache out of his joints,
    knock down her goddamn Kraut — *The man*,

his old woman used to plead, you *could be* —
        take his yacht keys, and the Benz keys, and *Good Lord,*
    Good Lord, go down on that angel of damnation.

DISSOLUTION

The cold waves douse the cove's waist still rimmed
with bare winter soil. It's difficult not to worry

when the sun wastes itself in the bracing air,
which is the Adriatic in early April.

Among tufts of grass, the primitive asparagus —
their wildness sticks out like first grey hairs:

one by the rock — and on its back a black snake
that, when disturbed, glides into the shrubs —

a few shoots swaying by the foot of the cypress,
and several steps farther, in the flattened green,

an animal's sockets. The sea-drift has polished,
bleached nearly, her hornless elongated head

into the smoothness of a porcelain urn.
And in their sleekness, their bride-like whiteness,

there's nothing to tell the grief of these bones.
Noble, like the world's first ghost, she holds on

to no struggle, except her stained teeth protrude
into this blunt unlife, her last motionless bite,

as the sea and the hollow karst go on with their needs,
the water's constant back-and-forth, the dissolution.

SARAJEVO CYCLE: 1992 TO 1996

After a while it became a routine: scrubbing laundry in the Miljacka,
stringing engine oil canisters to wheelbarrows or sleds,

or just holding them, like clusters of white balloons,
while edging down the rail of the bridge with the missing deck —

a wrinkled lineup swerving across that hollow stone arch,
down the bank, for the greasy plastic to gulp the river.

Up the waterside men cut oaks to stumps, spare the linden,
and trams, also hollow, rot stiff, their cables burnt worms.

Among anise and thistle stands a wheelchair, a wooly blanket is pulled
to a tarnished face, and a pair of chalky eyes gazes at a house sizzling.

Across the road, by a boarded-up *ćevabdžinica* joint, another man
sits and stares at the dust of his slippers, the bangle-folds of his socks.

A side street's lined with mortar and trash, and again a barrow:
100 Deutch Marks for a sack of firewood — the sack is hemp,

and the cart's tire is flat. There, a boy rides by on a bike, past a heap
of charred Yugos and Fiats, past the spray-painted, *Watch out. SNIPER*,

under a stream of facades aerated like chocolate — and one balcony
with dripping shirts, a carnation potted in a coffee tin.

The boy loops around the confetti of blown concrete in a courtyard
of a mosque, past fat-ankled women hoisting children down Heros' Square,

past men playing chess on the corroded hood of a Volkswagen, against
the backdrop of the bludgeoned courthouse, the toothless library,

past the fast-clacks through debris, clutched loaves of bread,
more *Run or R.I.P.* signs nailed to posts, the cyclist not heeding

the sickle-shape of a couple's legs on the sidewalk, or the child in a fuchsia
duffel coat with fingers curled in the red drool under her mouth,

up to the cemetery — the fermenting piles — where, a man in a tux,
with a cello stranded between knees, rubs the bow raw.

MEN FROM CAMPS

Postwar Bosnia

The world tried to find you on the map, maybe.
It's as if you slipped through some fault line, except
you did — dropped into pits, after squads fired in shifts.

Somewhere in the mists by the mountain tracks
and the guts of woods, the hairy blueweeds skirr
above the landfills of your remains —

your thin rooted arms, the fingers parched veins
of juniper, beech, needles of Bosnian Pine. The tilt
of your dried-moss heads wedged low in collarbones,

your turtled backs under sashed wrists: rope,
torn cloth, copper wire now loose. The missing.
Your hollow-drum eyes glare from behind blindfolds,

don't look up, or down. No more the truckloads of men,
the drills across barbed yards, the watery bean stew
before loading the bodies. No more hangars, or the smell

of the stalactites of blood under the execution stage.
Just you, your bits, femurs detached in transit, sticks
on the ground someone studies, identifies, like plants.

2. WHILE THE BACKWOODS BURNED

How when they wouldn't come out
I'd break their thin, coiled shells,

and I'd smoke, and the snails, primitive
and exposed, would trail long smears

on my palm, like down my throat,
its dark hollow, you leave yourself,

soured, into this woman whose town
is named River, who knows *bol*, pain,

when she sees it coming from Islam bol.

CROWS' VOICES

Rain sheets through the evacuated city,
hacks at gables, the siding of houses,

and the clustered black clouds ride low
over the corroded loops of rails, the roofs

that shift like synthetic bed covers.
Your vacant eyes soak the shuttered air,

our slumming. I rest my head on your shoulder,
and like sun in rye, palms laze in damp pubic hair.

Your fingers are thicker, cut by dirt like parsnips,
nails bitten to chipped bows. Hear that sugar-tap

of the plaster crumbling, the chair shouldering
your plaid shirt. The lights went off three days ago,

the sirens faded, stalled us in a blanket of heat
and the new habits our bodies assumed. The broken

circuitry, the monochromatic weather, the belting winds
that besiege this place, dismiss the new dawn: static,

unacceptable. And out there, through panels of slate gray,
in what's now a permanent dusk, this new familiarity —

the leathery voices of crows pass by like visitors,
each *kaah* and wheeze of their caws pulls the silk

of city drudgery toward the disheveled shores
where foam after barreled foam of each wave

escapes its own departure, and the late summer
unrolls with the thud of a musty rug.

MORE FERARUM

People are disappointingly human under the clothes they wear, but in
here, my sweet fickle angel, tricked by the side-casting moonlight

your shoulders turn to feathers rising through the indoor air. This
milky light, like latex leaking from opium fruit, pours across your face,

marks your pale chest. The arch of your instep, the hollows on either
side of your taut ass, the angle at which your arms meet elbows

are now just part man. Your locks, sweaty and smelling of metal, toss
and flash like moonhandled fish plunging through rapids.

Inexcusable, really, the voltage in the mud-spatter of your eyes as you
dive down, away from reason, ram into the barren valley of my bones.

GIFTS FOR THE PAST

Because you want to draw a portrait of me
wearing the two-pointed, coned island hat,

and you breathe, *Pose for me, my bare-shouldered*
Croat. I say, *yes*. I'll ask my people by the sea
to dig up the old seamstresses from the ground,

that because you want to render the Liburnian
in me, they'll have to make one last hat that peaks
like the sea brakes. It may take a while, though —

the old girls are asleep, breathless and bare-boned.
And let's not rush, no one wants to see them mad,
I say. But I don't tell you I ask for another hat,

or that I like dead women to wake up slowly,
to take their time rubbing their long fingers with sap,
and I don't tell you I want a portrait together —

black moon draped down your face, split cliff above mine —
because in the old portraits you had shown me,
your past bare-shouldered beauties stayed posing alone.

SKIRT DRIPPING SEA

The sky has been curdling for days —

            the slow-bloom of pale tumors
drifting against the oily lid of slate gray.

            Smoke tusks coil from burning leaf piles

and in treetops, unfurled black wigs,
            shallow nests gape emptied of sunlight.

The earth smells of whey and udders.

            There is no dust in winter, no weeping,
fish don't bark from tangled, slippery nets.

            Instead, the stethoscope-cold silence

and the buttery-gold glow of lichen
            furring over lifeless branches, stiff ropes,

their crusty flounce on aluminum hulls.

            And the wind that slices the leathery skin of the sea,
churns stale water in the hollows of boats,

            rattles the rigging metal like a coin in a dryer,

pulls the sails, slaps and swallows them,
            turns them into writhing disembodied tongues,

the urge to lick themselves. This wind,

its breath of sibilance and smoke, crass phosphorous
and bitter salt, of muck and smothered bark and tired sailcloth,

it wanders in through the door that's been left ajar —

grazes the wet skirt hanging on the wooden chair,
the worries that gathered in its folds, and nudges

your sex that is a flightless bird in a fallen nest.

SMALL CRIMES

A fence angled like a broken jaw,
mildew on rocks otherwise porcelain-white.

Blackthorns squat and daisies sway,
and the peasant's neck is bowed at the nape,

lined like a riverbed, his soul restored
in heat and salt. The mountain fakes ascension.

Its bare peaks jabbing the shifting sky
are what's left of its fallen state,

that, thick at its base, extends to the fields,
the lead-footed cattle. I step out of the car

by the roadside shrine — our black Madonna,
a plastic bouquet of stems at her dirty feet —

move closer to the man on the tractor
and the dieseled patchworks in caramel and bile:

flattened wheat and hops vines, empty hayracks.
I leave the door open, seats stained, worn smooth

like the ones in your car where last fall
I'd leaned toward you behind the wheel.

You stirred, semi-vigilant as I snapped the white buttons
on your shirt, undid the equator of your belt,

ducked from the eyes of people pushing carts
filled with cured lamb, corn on Styrofoam, cellophaned rye.

And as the last sprays of sunlight slid down
the hood of the sky, you shielded my black hair,

your hands familiar with churned earth,
and what it takes in the tucked back of a parking lot

to absolve a peopled afternoon of a small crime
and keep it hidden, keep it safe.

HOTEL SCANDINAVIA

We have a room, 208, in a hotel we never name —
someplace clean. Nordic. Perhaps Sweden. We tell stories,

like after the sun gives up, or never begins,
you knock and creep in with warm mugs of *glogg*.

Outside, northern winds throat through fells,
cluster trashed fir tips, blow whitecaps over crocheted lakes,

ice-crust fish left in the Arctic char. And under the milky down
our lazy feet, your erection, and expensive sheets.

Back home, in our Balkanized reality, elevators grate up
petrol-hued apartment prefabs, carry communal air

of fried peppers and pickled cabbage, news of heating riots,
and in the dockyard, buoys float like clotted fat on gravy.

Each evening you crouch on the oil-stained quay,
watch the sea tug at boat ropes, stars reflect on squat tankers.

Still, you see nothing but pale imagined snow.
Not a little like an affair — there isn't really a hotel —

just a state of life, a type of existence disguised as a hotel,
not more absurd than the strength of curved, lash-like ribs

of a ship, or the phantom weight of the lover's body.

WHEN AT MOONLIGHT YOU KNOCK ON MY DOOR

The first evening a man takes me to the movies, and as we walk out to his car, there waits a corroded Yugo, gone kaput long ago, and beside it, like a tall wilted lily grown out of the cracked sidewalk, his old father drips spleen. The following day I walk down a neighborhood street, and an old love walks towards me, runs his fingers through his thick black hair, waves, and as he comes closer, his eyes become burnt opium holes. *I'm wary of dreaminess in relationships*, I tell a friend. On the third night, I walk in a long line of people, up the side of a cliff on a narrow trail, and just as it bends into the woods, bombs start to rain like massive white chrysanthemums. We enter a large cave, walls smooth like snakeskin, and in that damp darkness, just as I start to miss the bombs, the lit-up sky, you appear, pull out a Kalashnikov, and as you take me farther underground, you belt out, *Nema više sunca*, there is no more sunlight, *nema više meseca*, no more moonlight.

WHILE THE BACKWOODS BURNED

Stories? I prefer what fits in two-or-three words, like not being scared.
Today nothing rhymes.

And the moon is pulling faces from the bottom of a coffee cup. Yesterday,
hearts thumped, then curdled, on the saucer.

Someone like you came around, friends say, loafed in front of Mom's house,
burned an extra cigarette at the seafront, just like that summer —

the smell of flaming tires, your waist in worn denim, my pinky hooked
around the belt loop, your palm under the burnt orange of my shirt, —
my dad's old shirt.

Those swallows that perched near the sea — they still come around.
Remember the dock, the city on the horizon? Knees going loose at 5 a.m.,
who stared the longest?

Don't pretend we had to move on. Listen. Swallows' songs linger. Their calls
are shorter. Simple as this.

AN OLD PHOTO OF YOU

The one snapped fast — your right hand
at the forefront, fending off the camera,
few forearm hairs, magnified and curled,
a shadow hanging over your unshaven face,
unswanky and red-eyed, half-lit on *loza*.

Now, I'd take your cheeks between the lines
of my palms, inhale by the slurring mouth,
unbutton that creased shirt, pull the worn-out cotton
over you, like snakeskin, the clasp of your
industrial-blue jeans giving in. Smoke would loom

thin, and your face would perk, brighten. I try to hear
now — it's almost real — that familiar voice, that face,
now opening feverish and full as Illyrian sky
lit with two smiling, drunk-moon eyes.

THIEVERY

Used to be bootleg tapes and bone bracelets
from vendors lining the promenade at Christmas.

Enameled bottle caps and cigarette lighters
with pictures of Our Lady of Lourdes. I pinched

sunflower seeds from Božo, the street peddler,
swiped hairpins from drugstore displays.

Between seizures, Koka's retarded uncle, Toni
used to rock in their den by the floor lamp,

like a Muslim bowing down on a prayer rug,
his 60-watt minaret glowing. Friday afternoons,

houses dazed after boiled chard and fried hake,
Koka and I would snatch his morphine and valium,

a handful of temazepam. Toni's dead now,
and so is Božo. The market's cleaned up, too —

the trinkets lost or broken. Tonight again
the gutters drool, and across the street

a man with a bedroll sits under the same chestnut
he's been sitting under for 25 years, sharing bread heels

with pigeons. A woman drifts by with a cart
of belongings, while in here, "Trouble Loves Me"

crashes against the walls, beats at my temples —
the needle-throb of that unflinching fact:

a man gone missing can't be taken. I wish the truth
would shrimp itself into a corner. Even then,

I smell you in my evening coffee, picture you at your desk:
fingers dug into hair, dark, shiny as rain-soaked turf —

wringing out words. And again, the scenario of desire
plays out: stealing weekends by that estuary,

where fresh water rushes into salt with relief,
like the pull of the yellow to a ripening lemon,

hazelnuts and shreds of honeycomb on back roads,
moss-covered ground and arms for pillows —

because no sin can stain the soil, because
I'll only let water hear the names you called me.

PLAINSONG WITH BULRUSH AND POPPIES

And the leaves drop on dirt roads with no
flamboyant or stately conclusions.

You and I, linked underarm, hiked
blind to passed towns, the swine in suits,

ditched clothes to wade through bulrush,
left morphine-white trails of dirty tales and rumors.

Was it the crunch of dried flower pods underfoot
that made the air seem dry? I could've carried you.

Or did you take a boat to some other shore?
Did you, like terns, turn to water for sustenance?

I toss dry soil over your picture now, slip a handful
of dirt into my breast pocket so we'd still be linked —

like the uprooted weed is linked to its desiccating sun,
or a coiled leaf that nourishes the ground.

HANDS

The woman with specks of ash in her hair
puts out cigarette butts in empty paint cans.

She is angular and her body's made hard.
In her stone house she listens to the weather.

Sometimes she salt-cures cod, stuffs squid,
and paints in her underwear. One, the image

of a house getting washed away by the sea,
a fallen grey tooth in a frothed mouth.

Two, unleavened bread on sunbaked soil.
Three, outside, on the back of a wooden chair

a pair of wide raven wings mid-flap —
and from one canvas onto another, as if

the tilt of the word depended on it, her hands
transfer the quiet of disconnected things.

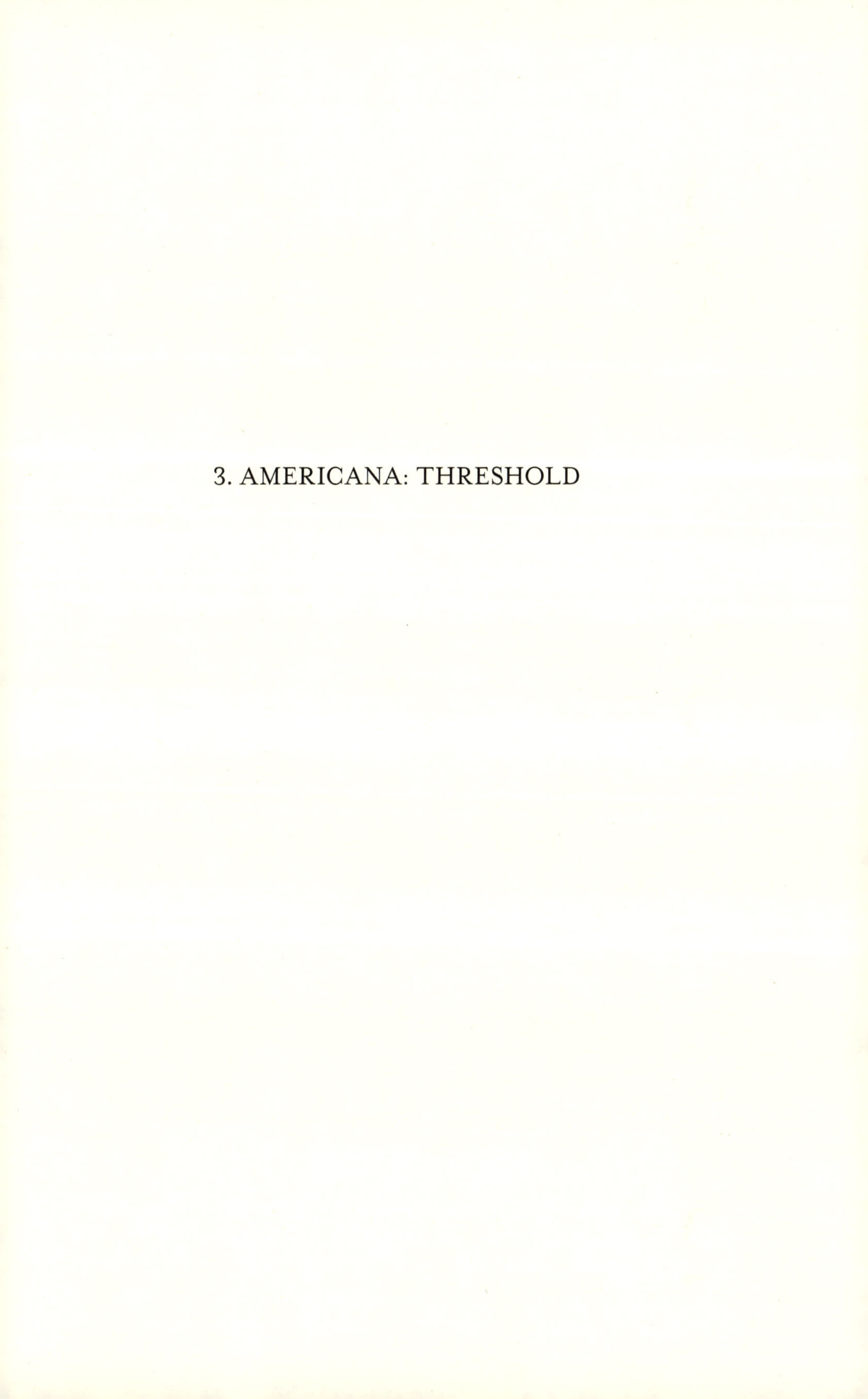

3. AMERICANA: THRESHOLD

LOVE BOAT

If I talk to it nicely, will it work? he asks
while scanning my card, feeling the strip

on its plastic back. I mumble back something
clumsy. He's cute, gives me long looks —

cheesy, but he thinks he's skillful.
His long forearms, their bulging veins

show under the rolled-up plaid shirt, its tail
tucked loosely below the ribs of his corduroys.

He's far too young, though, and I've fallen
for bookish types too many times before,

my history with such as necessary
as the scrawny poetry shelf in the corner.

Perhaps immigrants' histories should be pushed
overboard off some transatlantic ship, made illegal,

declined visa and residence and sent to Cuba. Start fresh.
But Cuban music is sensuality and vice fused tight,

and I imagine Creole nights must have that universal
sultry strum, mellow sounds cueing something more disturbing —

like jazz in movies signals a brooding scene:
a little room in the back, a bistro chair,

a swinging bulb, and someone beaten to a pulp,
a gutted mess of flesh, but the music's somehow sweet

like sugar stirred into bitter coffee,
and haunting like sorrow in a man's voice.

PEELING AN ORANGE

As the engine runs, you realize
    you were meant to be with her,
  at least one warm afternoon.

Like today. Imagine: right here,
    behind the soot-laden ashtray,
  a trail of notes, your oxford shirt,

the breath of her flimsy slip,
    your back arcing over her
  on the cracked leather seat —

the sun, torn, whether to burn
    or bleed over the wrinkled horizon.
  She's peeling an orange now.

You could stop the car,
    her fingers would lodge around
  your shoulder blades,

travel to where it hurts
    the most. Or you could keep driving,
  and there, in the distance,

beyond the carp of the city traffic,
    doused street lamps, past drab billboards
  and the woods, it'd be your cock,

not the orange, swelling in her hands.
    She'd overlook your lack of foreskin
  because, after all, you're American,

you're Route 66, well-trafficked and wide,
        and that eluding freedom of the West —
    she'd catch it, if only between her thighs.

You could pass Amarillo —
        the shrill-drone of cicadas piercing the heat —
    reach New Mexico, drive through Arizona

with the spirit of a mechanical bull.
        Just think, all the knee-tremblers
    against your coal-black Jeep,

tongue-on-breast rasps enough miles
        away from both of your homes
    neither would betray the local decorum.

And you, like any girl's first American boy
        should be — part astronaut,
  part cowboy, hair of ink and salty air,

you look at the orange rinds, say, *Nice scent.*
        Yes, she politely nods, *The accent, I mean,*
    is nothing to like or not.

BLUESMAN WEPT AND MIDNIGHT COULDN'T HIDE IT

The winter has straddled a dense stillness on the world
and the muslin curtain on the front door's broken pane
shifts and gasps like a petty neighbor. We're denned
in a borrowed one-bedroom, incognito, for a night
of wine-soggy Dixie cups and *Meet Me in the City,*
that, thick as condensed milk, drags along floorboards,
the morphine-white couch. And the blues — unpolished,
and sore — snags, like stockings, and stumbles like tongues
still new to each other. The backslide of the bass's drone
charges like packs of mourning buffalo — that steady,
pitiless earth-sway, Junior Kimbrough tears into *Please*
don't leave … and as he keeps repeating his small words,
and you clutch my neck pink, give way to the wolf-panting,
midnight clasps us to itself, tightens the moon in its cold jaw.

MEMPHIS AUBADE

Here, the Wolf and the Mississippi converge
into a signature. Down Union Avenue, slick with rain,

the cruising car keeps us above the anticipation,
leaves the riverfront and the bluffs in the dark, gears up

for what's become palpable. Placed on the tongue —
this drizzle, your name — are more ruthless tomorrows.

For the night, though, they're the crunch
of curing tobacco, air pockets in tumblers of scotch,

the longing sweep of the wah-wah pedal, its lingering
sweet spot. And now, darling, like the Chickasaw,

we've got nothing but the white fog that's entered
the torn seams of the quilt, the shadows clasping —

and in this absence of daylight, the non-elegance
of truth, the weight of twined limbs. Ask for nothing.

And hear: something, out the window, is strumming
the damp branches of lindens, their buds unseen.

SKEPTIC'S PRAYER

How to have faith in this thing, a new
man whose hands you've fallen into,

and in which you act as if nothing
of you is broken? As if this loving

doesn't make you feel pitch-high,
drenched and naked under the sky

that churns with flocks of night birds.
As if, while you edge his borders —

the scar above his lip, the inked
Reaper clutching the scythe tipped

into black soil, the drumming hymn
of his chest and the warmth of his

ass — as if you don't ache for the air
to remain this ripe, and like a square

skeptic act as if everything you say
isn't a prayer for the birds to stay.

AUBADE WITH THE MARKING SCENT OF TOBACCO, SWEAT, SORES

Dear, the anemone can't hear the wind,
and next to the herbs that spring and wilt,

women squat, the wings of their pelvises
low and wide as in childbirth. They never forget,

the old women, how the dogs yelped
while men's diamond-shaped hands

pawed across their small, walnut-like breasts,
pressed their backs against farmhouses,

marked slim tulip signets. How they understand,
embody, short-lived positions, how right now,

as they start to get up, bend over thyme, the wind
stoops the blue anemone and sweeps the ground,

the faint rustle of *I want, I want*, not different
than the waking lover, blunt through sleep.

I CLOSE MY HAND, STARS FALL THROUGH MY FINGERS

When sleep starts to fade out of your bodies,
and then you tire them again, no one knows

what happens next: desire insists, love doesn't.
And when you hear your lover's knuckles

tap griefless beats on your kitchen table,
when you notice that forgotten daylight

breaking inside your hollow chest, it's time
to turn away — drive into the known night,

away from the sounds that loosen your sinews,
leave your car at the edge of the damp woods,

and like a grown woman, palm your own
clenched fist, cling to your own shins,

but escape the urge to make your needy
hand grab the one that makes music for you.

PARTING

We hold onto this moment as if it were a paper boat

that we take from the warm bedroom out into the chill,

place in the shallow puddle by the trees' roots,

and like silent children we watch as if the boat's folds

will somehow resist the rain, won't go to pieces in the mud,

as if love is some imaginary silver sail — long, iridescent

and primitive — that cuts through the waters in which we drown.

ENGLISH LESSON

Your fingerprint — a clumsy poke
in the indigo-blue of his oil paint —

is dry now. The chocolate egg you eat
melts like a foreign word, and while he drawls,

in the silky voice of a sweeping brush,
the tip of his tongue loiters against his palate,

that pull of the dark *L* each time he calls you,
but not by your real name,

which is crowded with consonants,
but something more rounded, a syllabic wave

rolling through his mouth. He stretches his arm,
like when he would hand you his keys,

this time to take the scrunched wrapper,
then places it, a souvenir, on the black bookshelf,

beside frayed canvas spines and other wrappers —
hollow and supine like iridescent beetle husks —

and still, you adore that mouth,
slow when he talks, the swift strike of his kiss

and later, after the bites of anger,
you learn the word: cottonmouth.

UNTRANSLATABLE

The morning is dank. The mesh screen windows
of the Hot Fish diner sag heavy like hungover eyes,

and beneath them, draped across the green juniper,
the slow blink of Christmas lights offsets the fog.

Reed, washed-up weeds, and splinters of gray wood
scum the surface of the greasy, long-collapsed deck,

and while the wind hammers the chests of gulls,
the ocean recedes, falls back into its impassive self.

The sky hangs like strung flags, sloppy and wind-torn,
just as back in the house you nod, sink your thoughts

into the couch pillows, their white untranslatable stuffing,
and later you leave only a few silky hairs on the bathroom floor,

in the towel, a salty trace of your semen, a note, *Both demons*
and love can sneak up like an illness, make a man disappear.

SPARRING WITH UNANSWERED PHONE CALLS

Perhaps you're on a road trip with some busty American
who flaunts enough foreign blood to count for charm,

someone with no opinion on doves and shotguns,
her diction flawless even as her breath fogs up

your windshield. The asphalt stinks of rain now,
and the elm leaves don't shiver like that day

when they came down with something — something
perhaps to do with the syrup-thick August air. You said,

back then, you loved the pungent fern-scent of churned dirt,
and how, if you were in town, we'd be the river-mist

over the senseless lead of this city, lips like a delta
eddying from wrecking throats. Now, the tight gullet,

the spilt Dixie cup of affection, my gym of eclipses
where I punch blows, bare-knuckle hooks —

no partner, just me, my uppercut. Solitary, not as in sad,
or lonely. As in once, every goddamn elm was sick.

LAMENT WITH MILKWEED

I drive to the town where the room
waits ready for us. I know you can't make it.

Still, I need to see it,
brush my face against its sheets. Perhaps the room has answers —

331: acrylic curtains,
lead-white bedding, a panel of sunflowers, mirrored walls.

The door withdraws behind me,
and I, suitcase in hand, rooted in front of those mirrors

(you would've loved them),
reflecting a face slightly older than last I saw it —

the eyeliner, cracked a little,
like blacktop. I stand the rough rise of my breath,

its washboard stutter,
unbutton my coat, unzip the boots, the new dress,

stare at the reflection,
that shape of lame desire — and something about the air,

the cool tiles underfoot,
takes me to the icy rain that beat the milkweed stalks, mayhaws,

their branches silent
like hung pheasants, the bruised eye of the moon,

your Jeep plunging into the ditch,
bloodstain on the dash, you staggering the country roads for miles,

and on the ground
muddy rivulets gathering like hair pulled by a lover's hand.

POMEGRANATE

We never had much sun
in that last rented room,
the blacked-out window
the two wooden chairs
and the same old freckled
pomegranate we kept
slicing across trying
not to make the seeds bleed
but they always did. And
the pomegranate would
heal again and we'd
look at it — the fatal fruit
in the center of the room —
scratch our heads
from opposite corners,
wonder how to open
this small burning sun,
this little clenched fist
without breaking.

WHILE PAINTING A FALL LANDSCAPE, I IMAGINE

drifting off on this bed of fallen leaves,
        eye-level with a birch branch bowed low,
    the end of its gold limb dipped

into the creek, reflections both in and out
        of focus, angled like broken bottlenecks.

Startled awake, I wonder if thoughts
        can be harbingers. Did mine, just moments ago,
    sense this unexpected presence —

This knowing face suddenly leaning
        across the canvas, peering from the trees,

its bottomless gaze emerging
        from the wet skin of burnt sienna
    and linseed oil? Is this how you come back?

Your portrait paints itself? The creek
        starts to ripple now, then swirls into a rush

of soapy water, into that morning
        of your silhouette darkening the shower curtain,
    and the watch coming off my wrist.

NOCTURNE IN BLACK, AND LACY-RED ARILS OF NUTMEG

The elm casts a shadow on the lawn like a hunter carrying

limp-necked geese. I'm baking greens with cherry tomatoes,
russet potatoes with orange peppers for tomorrow.

It's not what these hands look after and put together,
but the mind that resembles a butcher's counter —
game breasts fingered, hollowed, cleaned.

I watch these hands I don't know: they wipe silver knives,
roll the pin across pine nuts sealed in a clear plastic bag,
cook crates of currants down into dark spoonfuls,

they crush cloves, break mace blades, stamp the yellow
out of lemons, lay black sesame seeds on rising buns,

two grieving fools, they freeze it all.

AUBADE

Forget the morning of the dead mouse
in the sink, the rust that the pipe coughed.
Swim off the dock. Pass the empty gangplank
and the mossed legs of anchors,
paddle through that water, sick for air,
and forget your lover's feet in your lap,
the half-light's illicit trace on the mandolin.
His drab couch. Forget your red handprint, patches
stitched to the curves of his black long johns.
Coming off, the prints deflating like soured fruit.
Forget the uneven legs of the three-drawer bureau
that held you. The muffled *hablar* of men
laying a roof in the alley behind the drawn blinds,
the way the shower water lashed as he said, *We'll always*
be this beautiful, then eddied as if deviled
by this casual sway — and look ahead past the lake,
at the backdrop, those wallpapered woods
where, you think, he took off, as wolves do.

BUFFALO MOON

That spring Tuesday after you packed, left your couch on the sidewalk, fog
entered its pulpy, pencil-shaved underbelly, its stained slender
frame.

If I had drunk myself to death that night, I would've liked you to carry me
to your river, lay our non-rescuable bodies

spread-eagle on its bank, tell me of the future: two people in an abject town,
asleep, the daybreak mimicking their spent bodies, white steam
rising from lichen-covered roofs.

Instead I dream stranded ships, how I drown caught in a mousetrap, how
we wear paper crowns and they burn — your brows, chin and lips
raw phosphorous. Your eyes, little black pits.

And I see you like that in the mornings sitting silently in the car beside
which I park. As I walk the streets, you pass by me. When I eat
you study my mouth,

when I sleep you tap my shins, wrists, wishbone hips, and I can't help say,
Give me your hand, touch, see how warm I'm down below.

THRESHOLD

Strange place I resist calling home — squat
on gray-painted brick foundations,
only the top half of the siding

in a fresh coat of pale yellow;
the rest, surrounding the tucked door
to the right, flaking like mammoth dandruff.

Four blistered black mailboxes,
all unnamed, the mossy gaps
in the leaning rail, and above it,

hanging off box nails: two fist-sized pots
hold faded geraniums —
both plastic and weightless

as they sway like spent debutantes.
They match the green porch carpet,
its rents along the edges

of the top step, and the kale-like curls
along the wall where it touches
my new front door.

I've been cleaning this place winter-long,
immersed in abrasion, in wiping
foot-rails with damp terry cloths.

Now each doorknob is polished —
brass, pewter and Bakelite.
Each shade, globe and shield

unscrewed from its fixture
        and the paper-like moths rinsed out,
                ribbons of settled dust

removed from the tops of doors.
        Paint stains, large, looking like pigeon
                droppings, scraped off tiles,

and the kitchen's grimy linoleum
        now bleached into paleness. And, as I bend
                and rise, my hands as if in oblation,

mimicking death and resurrection,
        I trace dirt and clay settled in the grout,
                cobwebs that waver complicit in corners.

Back and forth with the heel of my palm
        I try to remove time from the worn carpet,
                restore something in this house

perched over the two-lane road —
        uneven, rough, like sore taste buds —
                where trucks continually pass

and with them these camphor-white ceilings
        and the single panes shudder.
                Only traffic romps in here.

And across the street, children cry
        above this noise, learn to know
                their voices. And as I quietly wash,

all over again, each door in warm soap,
my hands wipe away the six hundred miles
between us, remember the borrowed houses

that hid us, hushed the billowing
inside them. I think of how right now
someplace boats are leaving their docks,

how easily they move — like the lifting
of eyelids, the sound of dawn, like breathing.
And with my hand sunk

into the wet sponge, I rub the doorframe,
firm as the curves of your shoulders,
and I clean, and we move together again.

GLOSSARY

barba *noun* (Piedmontese and Croatian dialect): uncle, man

boće *noun* (Croatian): bocce

briškula *noun* (Croatian): card game

ćevabdžinica *noun*: food joint that serves charcoal-grilled minced-meat **dish**, a type of kebab

dinar: Yugoslavian currency

Diocletian palace: ancient palace in the city of Split that was built by the Roman emperor Diocletian

Dobra pička (Croatian): Hot chick, lit: Good cunt.

džezva: pot for making Turkish coffee

Đelem, đelem: anthem of the Romani people

erotika *noun* (Croatian): erotica

glogg: mulled wine in Nordic countries

Goli otok: uninhabited island in north Adriatic, home of Yugoslavian political prison

hablar: *verb* (Spanish): talk

Jugo: warm, damp Mediterranean wind

kuna: Croatian currency

Kvarner: bay in the northern Adriatic

Les Quatre Cents Coups: 1959 film by Francois Truffaut

loza *noun* (Croatian): grappa, brandy

macchia *noun* (Italian): shrubs

Mamma Roma: 1962 film by Paolo Pasolini

Meet Me in the City: 1999 album by Junior Kimbrough, and its title song

Miljacka: small river in Bosnia that passes through the city of Sarajevo

Mirto *noun* (Italian): liquor made from the myrtle plant

nona *noun* (Croatian dialect, Italian: nonna): grandmother

nono *noun* (Croatian dialect, Italian: nonno): grandfather

No cazzo, ti resti qui. (Italian): No, dick, you stay here.

Plitvice: large national park in Croatia famous for its azure-blue lakes and subterranean karst rivers

pomodori pelati (Italian): peeled canned tomatoes

Pula: city on the southern tip of the Istrian peninsula, which is in northwest Croatia

Razbit ću ti pičku Ustašku. (Croatian): I'll break your fascist cunt.

Ronhill: Croatian cigarette brand

Sabrina: Italian pop singer known for her sexy looks and her 1987 hit "Boys"

štala *noun* (Croatian): stall, cowshed

"Trouble Loves Me": song from Morrissey's 1997 album *Maladjusted.*

Učka: mountain range on the Istrian peninsula in northwestern Croatia

Ustaše *noun* (Croatian): Croatian fascists in the 1930s and 1940s. Today the term is used for Croatian ultranationalists.

Vaffanculo *verb* (Italian): Fuck off.

Vukovar: city in eastern Croatia

ABOUT THE AUTHOR

Andrea Jurjević is a native of Croatia. Her poems, as well as her translations of contemporary Croatian poetry, have appeared in *EPOCH, TriQuarterly, Best New Poets, the Missouri Review, The Journal,* and *Gulf Coast*, among others. This is her first collection.